UNPLUG AND PLUG IN

A FUN GUIDE TO BOOST SELF-ESTEEM IN A SOCIAL MEDIA WORLD

UNPLUG AND PLUG IN

A FUN GUIDE TO BOOST SELF-ESTEEM IN A SOCIAL MEDIA WORLD

WORKBOOK FOR KIDS

DR. SHANIKA THOMAS, LCSW

Copyright © 2025 Dr. Shanika Thomas, LCSW

All rights reserved. No part of this publication may be reproduced, distributed, or transmitted in any form or by any means, including photocopying, recording, or other electronic or mechanical methods, without the prior written permission of the publisher, except in the case of brief quotations embodied in critical reviews and certain other noncommercial uses permitted by copyright law. For permission requests, write to the publisher, addressed "Attention: Permissions Coordinator," at the address below.

Paperback ISBN: 978-1-63616-252-2

Published By Opportune Independent Publishing Co.
www. opportunepublishing.com

Printed in the United States of America

For permission requests, please email the publisher with the subject line as "Attention: Permissions Coordinator" to the email address below:

Info@Opportunepublishing.com

To my son, Jeremiah, who is my daily motivation! Thank you for being the best son in the world! I love you.

Love, Mom

CONTENTS

A Letter to Grown-Ups	1
A Letter to Kids	3

All About Me and My Electronics

Social Media & Self-Esteem Pre-Test	5
Self-Awareness Test	7
All About Me!	8
S.M.A.R.T. Goal Tracker	10

CHAPTER ONE: *Understanding Social Media*

Social Media & Mental Health	12
Activity 1: Is It Safe?	13
Activity 2: My Safety Checklist	14
Activity 3: The Impact of Social Media	15
Activity 4: Emotions Check	16
Activity 5: Think Before You Post!	18
Activity 6: Scroll Smart!	19

CHAPTER TWO: *Healthy Habits*

Activity 1: Setting Boundaries with Screens	23
Activity 2: Online Etiquette	24
Activity 3: Billy the Bully	25
Activity 4: Let's Talk About It!	26
Activity 5: Scroll, Swipe, Solve	28
Activity 6: N.B.A. — New, Boundaries, Always	30

CHAPTER THREE: Pause Before You Post

How the Brain Works: Thoughts vs. Feelings	33
Activity 1: Mood Mix Up: Unscramble the Feelings!	34
Activity 2: Social Media Snapshot	35
Activity 3: Social Media Smarts	36
Activity 4: Social Media Boundaries Quiz	37
Activity 5: Circle of Control	40
Activity 6: Play Nice Crossword Puzzle	42

CHAPTER FOUR: Boost Your Self-Esteem

Activity 1: Be a Safety Superhero	46
Activity 2: Game Time, Guess Who?	47
Activity 3: Stop, Think, Reflect!	48
Activity 4: Who Am I …Without Social Media?	49
Activity 5: The Real Me, Offline!	50
Activity 6: The Offline Version of Me	51
Activity 7: You Matter, Be You!	53
Activity 8: The "Real Me" Checklist	54

CHAPTER FIVE: Who Am I Without Social Media?

Activity 1: Offline Fun Bingo Game	57
Activity 2: More Than Likes and Followers!	60
Activity 3: My Affirmation Wall	62
Activity 4: Spot the Fake!	63
Activity 5: Real Vs. Fake	66
Activity 6: My World, My Rules!	67
Activity 7: Touchdown With Confidence Maze	69

CHAPTER SIX: *Unplug and Celebrate Me!*

Activity 1: Cut It Off — 73
Activity 2: My Voice Matters! — 75
Activity 3: My Digital Footprint — 79
Activity 4: My Self-Care List — 81
My Online Safety Tips — 82
My Unplugged Activities List — 83
The Road to 'Unplug and Plug In' — 85

CONGRATULATIONS!

Post-Test: Social Media & Self-Esteem — 89
My Workbook Reflection — 91
Score Guide for Pre/Post-Test — 92
Answer Key — 93
Certificate of Completion — 94
Reference — 95

A LETTER TO GROWN-UPS

Welcome to the *Unplug and Plug In Workbook for Kids*. I'm Dr. Shanika Thomas, a licensed clinical social worker and school social worker. Since 2013, I've been helping children strengthen their emotional health.

This workbook guides kids to step back from social media, protect their well-being, and "plug in" to positive goals, activities, and joy. It teaches responsible online use, self-esteem, and safety, while reminding them that likes and comments don't define their worth.

Designed to be simple and engaging, it sparks conversation, builds confidence, and supports both literacy and social-emotional growth with your involvement making the biggest difference.

HOW TO SUPPORT YOUR SCHOLAR THROUGH THIS WORKBOOK:

- Read and talk together
- Provide a safe, honest space
- Celebrate progress, not perfection
- Share your own unplugging habits
- Encourage positive self-talk
- Check in on feelings regularly

This workbook supports social-emotional learning and healthy self-esteem for children navigating social media, but it is not a substitute for therapy or professional mental health care.

Please review the signs below to see if your child may need additional support:

- Ongoing sadness, hopelessness, or withdrawal for more than two weeks
- Loss of interest in hobbies, school, or play
- Major changes in sleep or appetite
- Low self-worth or self-harm statements
- Frequent frustration, mood swings, or trouble managing emotions
- History of trauma, bullying, or loss

If you notice any of these, contact a licensed therapist, school counselor, social worker, or pediatric mental health professional. Early support can make a big difference.

While this workbook is a valuable tool for starting conversations, building healthy habits, and developing social media smarts, mental health concerns deserve professional attention when needed.

A LETTER TO KIDS

Hi,

My name is Dr. Shanika Thomas. I help kids feel better about themselves, fix hard problems, and grow at school, and in life.

I am excited you have chosen to work independently or with a trusted adult to learn how to manage your feelings while using social media. This children's workbook, *Unplug and Plug In,* will help you step back from your electronics when things become too much. You will learn how to balance screen time while focusing on hobbies and goals. I want you to remember that likes, comments, and shares don't define your worth. You are awesome, just the way you are.

When reading this book, you can do it all at once or little by little; it is your choice. When you're all done, you will feel empowered to use social media with confidence, and don't worry, I will be with you every step of the way.

Now, let's get started. It's time to plug in!

With gratitude,
Dr. Shanika Thomas, LCSW

ALL ABOUT ME AND MY ELECTRONICS

SOCIAL MEDIA & SELF-ESTEEEM PRE-TEST

Fill in the blank with the best word or idea that fits. Do your best, there are no wrong answers!

1. One way I can protect myself online is by setting healthy _____ with people I talk to on social media.
2. Social media can be fun, but it can also affect the way I feel about my _____.
3. It's important to take breaks from my phone or gaming system so I can take care of my _____ and feelings.
4. Before I post something online, I should ask myself if it is _____ and _____.
5. When someone is being mean or hurtful online, that is called _____.
6. Not everything I see on social media is real. Some pictures are edited or _____ to look perfect.
7. Being kind online is called using good _____.
8. I can tell if a person is trustworthy online by looking for _____ signs and thinking carefully before I share anything.
9. The digital world means everything I do online leaves a _____, so I should always think before I click.

10. If there were no social media, I would spend more time _____ or doing things like _____.
11. When I feel left out or jealous of something I see on social media, I can help myself feel better by _____.
12. I know I am being true to myself online when I post things that make me feel _____ and _____.
13. If a stranger messages me online and it feels uncomfortable, I should _____ and talk to a trusted _____.
14. Social media doesn't show the full story of someone's life, so remind myself not to _____ myself to others online.
15. Being confident online means I don't need to post just to get _____ or _____.

SELF-AWARENESS TEST

Read each prompt on the left and quickly write down the first thought that comes to mind in the blank space on the right.

I am a Student who …

loves	
wants to	
enjoys	
is inspired by	
has a habit of	
is happiest when	
believes in	
would give	
will one day	
has the goal of	
believes in	
wakes up, then	
can't live without	

How many times did you mention social media or electronic devices in your "Self-Awareness Test" activity?

_____

ALL ABOUT ME!
Finish the sentences below.

I can _____

I like _____

I feel _____

I love _____

I need _____

I have _____

I am scared of _____

I dream of _____

My best friend is _____

My favorite animal is _____

My favorite food is _____

SPECIFIC: Describe your goal in detail.

MEASURABLE: List the measures you will use to track your goal.

ATTAINABLE: List the actions you need to take to reach your goal.

RELEVANT: Describe why this goal is worth achieving.

TIMED: Write the date you will achieve this goal by.

UNDERSTANDING SOCIAL MEDIA

SOCIAL MEDIA AND MENTAL HEALTH

Have you ever left school feeling super excited to grab your phone or tablet to check out what's happening on social media?

Maybe you couldn't wait to see all the posts and updates you missed! Or, have you ever had your parent take away your device and felt like you were missing out on the latest news or gossip?

If you answered "yes" to either of these, you're not alone! These are normal feelings we all get when we're hyped about the things we enjoy.

Here's something important to think about: What happens when the things we enjoy become distractions or put us in an unsafe situation?

That's why it's so important to understand social media and how it affects us.

 # IS IT SAFE?

What are your thoughts? Social media can be a tool for a lot of *positive* things, like making money, creating content, and connecting with family and friends. However, if you do not practice positive safety measures, then it can become unsafe.

Check "YES" or "NO"

DID YOU KNOW IT IS NOT WISE TO GIVE OUT YOUR PERSONAL INFORMATION ONLINE TO STRANGERS?	 
DID YOU KNOW WHEN YOU POST PICTURES OR VIDEOS ONLINE, THEY CAN BE THERE FOREVER?	 
DID YOU KNOW THAT TOO MUCH SOCIAL MEDIA CAN POSSIBLY CAUSE MENTAL HEALTH CHALLENGES?	 

However, *negative* use of social media can lead to cyberbullying, harassment, and exposure to inappropriate or harmful content, including violence and explicit material. So let's create a safety checklist to help guide us in remaining safe and in control.

MY SAFETY CHECKLIST

TIPS FOR STAYING SAFE ON SOCIAL MEDIA

Check the boxes you feel are most important to you.

- ☐ Use the block feature if you do not want to talk to someone

- ☐ Change your privacy settings to a private account

- ☐ Openly communicate and report bullying to a trusting adult

- ☐ Continue to be educated on online safety

- ☐ Being monitored to make sure I am okay

- ☐ Parents using parental control so I can be safe

- ☐ Learn responsible online behavior

WHAT'S ANOTHER METHOD TO REMAIN SAFE ONLINE?

THE IMPACT OF SOCIAL MEDIA

Did you know that social media can affect your feelings and emotions? It's true!

What are some feelings you feel when you use social media?

_____

_____

Is it positive or negative feelings? _____

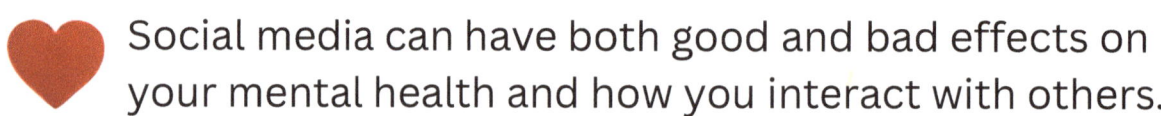 Social media can have both good and bad effects on your mental health and how you interact with others.

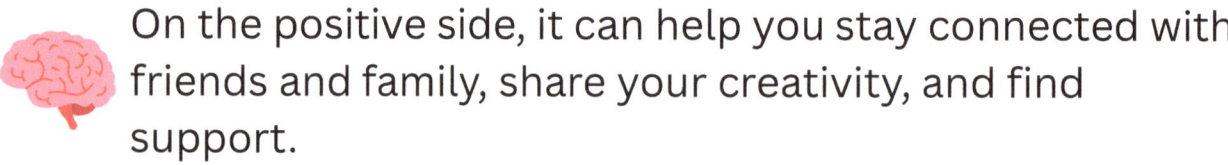 On the positive side, it can help you stay connected with friends and family, share your creativity, and find support.

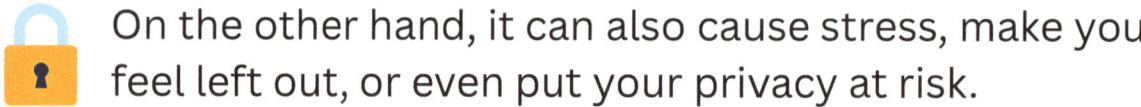 On the other hand, it can also cause stress, make you feel left out, or even put your privacy at risk.

That's why it's super important to understand how to use social media safely, how it can make us feel, and how to protect ourselves when we're online.

EMOTIONS CHECK

LET'S DO A QUICK CHECK-IN:

Circle some of the potential negative impacts you feel when scrolling on social media or have felt before. Please don't worry, this is not a quiz, and you won't get a grade.

- Cyberbullying
- Body image issues
- Low self-esteem
- TALKING TO STRANGERS ABOUT PERSONAL INFO
- DISTURBANCE OF SLEEP
- A lot of screen time
- Gossiping
- Sadness due to lack of likes
- Less time with outside play
- LONELINESS
- Anxiety
- Less time playing with other fun games
- SOCIAL ISOLATION
- "Fear" of missing out

Now, circle some of your potential positive impacts below.

THINK BEFORE YOU POST!

M	N	G	V	H	T	N	A	X	M	G	S	W	F	Y
O	C	K	T	S	A	O	U	Y	U	C	S	R	C	D
J	M	G	I	N	G	W	F	F	L	Q	J	S	Q	P
K	E	P	A	N	F	O	V	F	O	U	A	K	A	Y
I	S	H	Q	X	D	R	Y	O	Q	F	W	D	R	D
A	S	V	S	D	X	N	Y	E	E	W	W	C	S	P
E	A	N	U	Y	G	U	E	T	L	D	I	H	C	R
Q	G	Z	U	X	T	K	Y	S	E	D	A	V	F	O
O	E	O	J	O	L	H	B	Z	S	R	M	X	M	S
F	S	C	S	J	I	P	I	L	I	B	D	B	H	L
F	T	R	A	P	K	V	V	N	O	F	V	O	Y	F
I	G	J	U	X	E	Y	G	W	K	C	C	M	R	Y
O	P	P	K	A	S	T	T	R	S	I	K	X	D	Z
X	C	E	Y	R	B	F	H	O	A	H	E	I	R	U
R	E	S	P	E	C	T	I	H	O	D	N	Y	B	F

BLOCK   SHARING
MESSAGES THINK
RESPECT SAFETY
KINDNESS LIKES

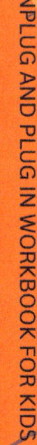

18

SCROLL SMART!

It's check-in time! Are you making smart choices when you scroll on social media? Fill out this worksheet, then we'll chat about it.

1 Which social media platforms do you use most?

2 What are things you enjoy or find positive about social media?

3 Are there things on social media that make you feel sad?

4 Do you feel safe when you talk to different people on social media?

5 When you are online, do you show up as the real you or a different side?

6 Describe how electronics affects your behavior and moods.

7 Are there any changes you would like to make in your use of social media?

SELF-ESTEEM & MOOD TRACKER

Let's track your mood to see how you are feeling after learning about the topics in this lesson:

Check the circle that describes how you feel right now.

Did you use social media today: (Yes or No) _____

How did it make me feel? _____

Let's track your self-esteem to see how you feel about yourself and your confidence: *Circle which best describes you.*

- I feel good about myself.
- I feel unsure.
- I compared myself to others.
- I feel proud of something I did.
- I didn't feel like "enough" today.

CHAPTER 2

HEALTHY HABITS

SETTING BOUNDARIES WITH SCREENS

Why do we have rules?
Imagine a world without any control, Chaos! Right? Rules help keep order, protect us, and make life safer. Boundaries with your electronics and social media do the same thing.

Why Boundaries Matter
Just like traffic laws protect drivers, online boundaries protect you from bad things happening and help you keep control in life. Setting limits on screen time helps you avoid distractions and leaves room for school, sports, hobbies, and time with friends and family.

TOO MUCH SCREEN TIME CAN:

- Hurt your eyes
- Keep you from sleeping well
- Take away time from real-life fun
- Cause cramps in your neck and back
- Affect your mood and mental health

Have you ever felt this way? (yes or no) _____
If yes, what happened?
_____
_____

ONLINE ETIQUETTE

Boundaries also show others how to treat you online. They remind you to:

- ✅ Use kind and respectful language
- ✅ Be careful with tone (ALL CAPS can sound like YELLING!)
- ✅ Think before you post! People can take your words differently than you meant.

Kindness
Boundaries encourage positive communication. They help you build respect and avoid misunderstandings, which makes online spaces friendlier and healthier.

Cyberbullying
Conflicts can happen online. Without boundaries, it's easy to get caught up in gossip, teasing, or excluding others. Online etiquette teaches you to pause, show empathy, and think about how your words might affect someone's feelings.

The Bottom Line:
Boundaries encourage positive communication. They help you build respect and avoid misunderstandings, which makes online spaces friendlier and healthier.

BILLY THE BULLY

Please read the story or ask an adult to read it with you.

While you read:
1. *Circle the words that show how Billy is feeling.*
2. *Underline the actions he takes when he's upset.*

In class, the teacher told everyone to finish their math work, then she heard a whisper. The teacher asked, "Who was talking?" and the entire class said, "Billy!" Billy got in trouble for talking in class, and his teacher called his mom because he yelled back, saying, "It was not me," angrily, and threw his paper on the ground. His mom said she would take his phone and video games when he gets home. Billy felt embarrassed. At recess, he sat alone, feeling mad. His friend asked, "Are you okay?" but he yelled at her, "Leave me alone." Then, he went online and posted a mean message on his page, left rude comments on other people's posts, and shared a meme making fun of his friend. Billy felt frustrated and sad.

Time to Reflect:

How do you feel about Billy's actions? Did he make a good choice?

LET'S TALK ABOUT IT!

Have you ever felt mad like Billy?

How did you feel, and what did you do?

Did Billy make a good decision?

What could he have done differently?

Have you ever done something you regret because you were mad? What was it?

SCROLL, SWIPE, SOLVE

Sometimes, being online feels like a lot of drama, rumors, and mean moments. Maybe someone posted something rude, slid into your DMs with hurtful words, or even dropped a diss track that feels like it's about you.

Ouch! That stuff really hurts.

**YOUR FEELINGS MATTER!
YOUR VOICE MATTERS!
YOU MATTER!**

Even as a kid, your emotions are real, and it's okay to not be okay, feel sad, angry, or even confused.

Have you ever had someone be mean to you online, like sending hurtful DMs or leaving rude comments? _____

How did it make you feel?
_____

LET'S GO DEEPER

Describe how you should respond to each scenario.

I posted pictures every day this week on my social media account, and my best friend didn't "like" or "comment" on all my posts, so I started questioning our friendship.

Was this a smart decision? _____
_____

I let my cousin use my social media account while she was on punishment. She messaged a classmate I don't like, and now the classmate has reported me to the principal.

Was this a smart decision? _____
_____

A boy in my class made a diss song. Since he used the first letter of my name, I thought it was about me. I got mad, made my own diss song, and posted a mean picture of him. He told his mom, and she reported me to the school.

Was this a smart decision? _____
_____

This next activity is a fun game that will help you learn what it means to have resilience, which is a fancy word for bouncing back after tough online moments.

TRAIN LIKE A DIGITAL CHAMPION

Just like NBA players practice, train, and bounce back after tough games, you can train your mind to stay strong online!

Even when things get tough, like a rude comment, being left out of a group chat, or comparing yourself to someone else, you can bounce back and keep going.

Let's get to the gym so you can build your confidence and bounce back to become a digital champion!

Pick your basketball team: _____

Pick your player: _____

Pick the position: _____

LET'S RUN SOME DRILLS

N.B.A. STANDS FOR

NEW
Try a healthy new habit online.

Write one new habit you want to start.
Example: log off before bed or say something kind online

☐

BOUNDARIES
Know when it's time to take a break.

Write one online boundary you will start today.
Example: no social media during homework or set an online time limit

☐

ALWAYS:
Always bounce back, even after a tough moment.

What will you do if someone posts something mean about you?
(Circle one you can try today)

Talk to an adult   Log off   Play a board game   Go outside

SELF-ESTEEM & MOOD TRACKER

Let's track your mood to see how you are feeling after learning about the topics in this lesson:

Check the circle that describes how you feel right now.

Did you use social media today: (Yes or No) _____

How did it make me feel? _____

Let's track your self-esteem to see how you feel about yourself and your confidence: *Circle which best describes you.*

- I feel good about myself.
- I feel unsure.
- I compared myself to others.
- I feel proud of something I did.
- I didn't feel like "enough" today.

CHAPTER 3

PAUSE BEFORE YOU POST

HOW THE BRAIN WORKS: THOUGHTS VS. FEELINGS

Your brain is amazing, and it helps you feel things and think things! But sometimes, feelings can be so big and fast that they make you want to act right away, especially when you're on social media.

THOUGHTS

Thoughts help you slow down and think things through before you react. You should always THINK FIRST!

FEELINGS

Feelings happen quickly! The way you think about something can change the way you feel.

HAVE YOU EVER NOTICED?

If you think 'I can't do this,' you may feel sad, but if you think 'I'll try,' you may feel brave.

When feelings take over, you might post or compare without meaning to, but if you pause and think first, you can make better choices, stay out of trouble, and feel proud of yourself.

LET'S PRACTICE

Think about the difference between your thoughts and feelings before completing the activity on the next page.

MOOD MIX UP:
Unscramble the Feelings!

1. PPYHA _____
2. ASD _____
3. ASINXUO _____
4. AGYRN _____
5. CEFDNTION _____
6. YDRNEFLI _____
7. SDSEERST _____
8. OUHRM _____
9. AXELR _____
10. OELVD _____
11. NINETACUR _____
12. ERNUCIES _____
13. EMWDLHEOERV _____
14. EIRDROW _____
15. LETF TOU _____
16. ULEFHCER _____
17. SSEESTDR UTO _____
18. AONTADIV _____
19. OELNLY _____
20. DERBO _____
21. CMLA _____
22. BREAV _____
23. ETCDIEX _____
24. SPATDNPEIOI _____
25. SRSUPEDRI _____

SOCIAL MEDIA SNAPSHOT

A DAY IN MY SOCIAL MEDIA LIFE:

_____

_____

_____

MY SOCIAL MEDIA MOOD:

_____

_____

_____

MY SOCIAL MEDIA HABITS:

_____

_____

_____

SOCIAL MEDIA SMARTS

My Current Online Boundaries: Let's be completely honest and have a discussion.

Do you tell your parents about what you do on social media?

_____

_____

Do you have any boundaries on social media?

_____

_____

Do you tell your business or someone else's business on social media?

_____

_____

Let's quiz your social media boundaries.

1. Do you feel comfortable saying "no" if someone asks you for personal information or an inappropriate picture?
    a. Yes
    b. No
    c. Sometimes

2. When someone sends you a message or comment that makes you feel uncomfortable or upset, do you know how to block, report, or talk to a trusted adult?
    a. Yes
    b. No
    c. Sometimes

3. Do you take long extended breaks from social media to focus on enjoyable activities, like hobbies, sports, or spending time with family and/or friends offline?
    a. Yes
    b. No
    c. Sometimes

4. If someone online is being mean or bullying others, do you feel confident about reporting it to a trusted adult and/or utilizing the report feature on social media?
    a. Yes
    b. No
    C. Sometimes

MY SOCIAL MEDIA BOUNDARIES SCORECARD

INSTRUCTIONS

Let's add up the points!

If you answered "Yes" to any of the questions on the last page, give yourself 3 points.

If you answered "Sometimes," give yourself 2 points.

If you answered "No," give yourself 1 point.

Add up your points to see how well you're setting boundaries on social media!

WHAT IS YOUR SCORE?

_____

WHAT DOES YOUR SCORE SAY ABOUT YOU?

If your score was 10–12 points: You're doing a great job setting strong boundaries on social media! Keep it up and keep reading this book so you can set even more boundaries.

If your score was 7–9 points: You're on the right track, but there may be a few areas where you can improve. Think about how you can strengthen your boundaries. I will help you! Keep reading this book.

If your score was 4–6 points: It might be time to talk to a trusted adult about how to set stronger boundaries online. Setting limits and knowing when to report or block can help you stay safe. You are not alone! Keep reading this book to learn more.

If your score was 3 points or less: It's really important to learn how to set boundaries on social media to protect your feelings and privacy. Talk to a trusted adult to get some tips and start working on your boundaries today! It's not too late. Keep reading so you can learn the dos and don'ts of setting boundaries on social media and keeping yourself safe.

Are you surprised by your score? _____

What would you like to change moving forward?
_____
_____

CIRCLE OF CONTROL

Is setting healthy boundaries tough for you? Do you have a hard time saying, No! Or maybe you have a tough time ignoring drama or messy situations. Let's identify the things in your life that you feel are in and outside of your control.

Do you need an example? Okay, I will go first. One thing that is out of my control is the internet connection. Like, if I lose power right now, that is out of my control, and the only possible way for me to fix it is to contact my internet carrier.

One thing that is in my control is the amount of time I spend on social media because I can put my phone or tablet down and pick up a book. Okay, now it's your turn.

OUT OF MY CONTROL	IN MY CONTROL

40

JOURNAL ENTRY:
How can you set boundaries with your Electronics?

Think about ways you can learn how to manage your screen time, set limits, and prioritize your well-being. Can you spend time learning a new skill or enjoying other hobbies?

PLAY NICE
ONLINE ETIQUETTE, KINDNESS, AND CYBERBULLYING

CROSSWORD PUZZLE

ACROSS

4. A good friend online and in real life should always act?
5. If someone is bullying you online, you should ell an?
6. To stop negative interactions online, you can use the feature to prevent someone from contacting you.
8. The way we act and communicate respectfully online is called?
11. You should never share your full name or address online to stay?
12. Instead of comparing yourself to others online, you should focus on your own?
14. If you see someone being bullied online, you should not join in but instead?
15. Leaving a nice comment or compliment on someone's post is an act of?

DOWN

1. If social media makes you feel bad, you should take a?
2. When something is posted online, it can stay there?
3. A safe way to protect your personal information is to adjust your?
7. Being mean, spreading rumors, or embarrassing someone online is called?
9. What should you do before posting something online?
10. Spreading information online about other people is called?
13. You should treat others and yourself online with?

SELF-ESTEEM & MOOD TRACKER

Let's track your mood to see how you are feeling after learning about the topics in this lesson:

Check the circle that describes how you feel right now.

Did you use social media today: (Yes or No) _____

How did it make me feel? _____

Let's track your self-esteem to see how you feel about yourself and your confidence: *Circle which best describes you.*

- I feel good about myself.
- I feel unsure.
- I compared myself to others.
- I feel proud of something I did.
- I didn't feel like "enough" today.

DID YOU KNOW?

The definitions of confidence and self-esteem seem similar, but they really mean different things!

SELF-ESTEEM is how much you value and care about yourself.

Example: You feel good about who you are, even if you don't win the game or ace the test.

CONFIDENCE is believing in what you can do.

Example: "I know I can score two touchdowns," or "I believe I'll pass my next test."

Self-esteem reminds you that you're valuable no matter what, while confidence helps you trust your abilities to reach your goals.

BE A SAFETY SUPER HERO

CONFIDENCE VS. SELF-ESTEEM

Welcome to The League of Inner Strength, where our superheroes help kids like YOU understand the awesome power inside of you.

 Understanding the difference between confidence and self-esteem!

 Captain Confido: He's not afraid to try new things! Whether juggling flaming watermelons or presenting projects in front of his class, he tries, even if he messes up.

The Amazing Esteema: She knows she's valuable, no matter what! Even if she isn't that good in math or misses her 3-point shot in a basketball game, she still believes she's awesome.

SO, WHAT'S THE DIFFERENCE?

LET'S BREAK IT DOWN:

CONFIDENCE

"I know I can do this!"

"I've got the talent!"

"I can do well on the test."

SELF-ESTEEM

"I'm still great, even if I can't."

"I believe I am worthy."

"Even if I didn't, I am still a good person."

Now, it is your turn to try:

_____ _____

_____ _____

GAME TIME, GUESS WHO?

Match the quote to the correct superhero! Write the word "confidence" or "self-esteem" under the quote it belongs to.

1
"I can learn how to ride my bike if I keep trying!"

_____

2
"If I don't get the grade I wanted, I'm still proud of myself for trying."

_____

3
"I don't know how to cook yet, but I'm going to try!"

_____

4
"I'm still cool, even if I don't win the soccer game."

_____

STOP, THINK, REFLECT:

1. What's something you feel confident doing?

2. What's something you're not great at, but you still feel good about yourself anyway?

3. Can you think of a time when your self-esteem helped you bounce back from a mistake or a poor decision?

WHO AM I...
WITHOUT SOCIAL MEDIA?

If social media disappeared, how would you feel?

Who would you become?

How would people view you in real time if you could not post your happy moments?

DID YOU KNOW?

In 1995, the social networking platform Classmates.com was launched, followed by SixDegrees.com in 1997. In the early 2000s, the world used other popular platforms like Friendster, MySpace, and LinkedIn. Have you ever heard of any of these platforms before?

THE REAL ME, OFFLINE!

LET'S EXPLORE YOUR IDENTITY BEYOND YOUR SOCIAL MEDIA PROFILE.

What do you usually share online? (i.e., friends, family, hobbies)

_____

_____

If I were to pull up your social media account right now, what would I see?

_____

_____

Do you think your social media shows the full version of who you are?

_____

_____

What are some things about you that people don't see online?

_____

_____

Are there parts of you that you hide or change for social media?

_____

THE OFFLINE VERSION OF ME
LET'S GET BACK TO THE BASICS

"These things are true about me, even if I never post about them."

I am good at:

_____

_____

Something I've overcome is:

_____

_____

If I couldn't post a picture ever again, I'd still:

_____

_____

YOU ARE AMAZING!
WITH OR WITHOUT ELECTRONICS

You are an amazing kid, with or without your electronics. Your value doesn't come from likes, followers, or comments. It doesn't come from filtered pictures. It comes from your self-awareness, your choices, your beliefs, and who you are when no one is watching.

Self-awareness means knowing what makes you, YOU! It is your thoughts, feelings, strengths, likes, dislikes, values, and even how you react to things.

When we're always on electronics or social media, it's easy to get distracted from our real selves and our real lives. We start believing we have to act, look, or have a certain behavior online.

However, self-awareness helps you remember who you are when the phone is off, the games are paused, no gossip, tea, or drama, and just...YOU.

YOU MATTER, BE YOU!

WHY DOES IT MATTER?

Social media can blur the line between what we like and what we think we're supposed to like.

The more self-aware we are, the stronger our self-esteem becomes, because we aren't depending on other people to tell us who we are. Without electronics, we can better notice what we truly enjoy, value, and believe, not what's just trending online.

DEVELOP YOUR OWN TRENDS!

How do you act when you're around close friends or family vs. online?

_____

_____

What are 3 words used to describe your real personality?

_____

_____

_____

When do you feel most like yourself?

_____

_____

THE "REAL ME" CHECKLIST

Check the best answer(s)

MY STRENGTHS

- ☐ I'm a good friend.
- ☐ I'm creative.
- ☐ I try to do hard things.
- ☐ I help others in need.
- ☐ I'm funny and kind to others.

THINGS I LIKE (NO SCREENS)

- ☐ Reading a book
- ☐ Playing sports
- ☐ Drawing or creating
- ☐ Being outside
- ☐ Talking with family
- ☐ Building things, solving puzzles, or playing board games

HOW I HANDLE MY FEELINGS

- ☐ I talk to someone I trust.
- ☐ I take a break.
- ☐ I write or draw.
- ☐ I go outside.
- ☐ I keep it in and don't know what to do yet. (That's okay, too — we're learning!)

Stop, Think, Reflect

The more you know yourself, the stronger your confidence becomes. You don't need a screen to discover what makes you special and unique.

SELF-ESTEEM & MOOD TRACKER

Let's track your mood to see how you are feeling after learning about the topics in this lesson:

Check the circle that describes how you feel right now.

Did you use social media today: (Yes or No) _____

How did it make me feel? _____

Let's track your self-esteem to see how you feel about yourself and your confidence: *Circle which best describes you.*

- I feel good about myself.
- I feel unsure.
- I compared myself to others.
- I feel proud of something I did.
- I didn't feel like "enough" today.

CHAPTER 5

WHO AM I WITHOUT SOCIAL MEDIA?

OFFLINE FUN: WHO AM I?
BINGO GAME

This fun game will help you reflect on who you are beyond social media. It encourages you to focus on your strengths, interests, and unique traits offline. Complete five activities in a row on the next page to **WIN**!

Write down three things you love about yourself that have nothing to do with how you look.	Describe a recent accomplishment you feel proud about and did not share it on social media.	Think of a talent or skill you have that isn't showcased online.	Write about a time you felt truly present and happy, without any distractions from social media.	Share a time you felt the most happiness and did not share it on social media.
Describe a time you did something creative that didn't involve screens (e.g., drawing, journaling, cooking).	List five things you enjoy doing offline (no technology) that bring you joy.	What are three things you are involved in at school or in the community that does not involve electronics?	Reflect on what you want to be known for, beyond your social media presence.	List 5 adjectives that describe your personal strengths or characteristics.
When is the last time you volunteered, or helped someone and did not post it to social media?	Write down one thing you're grateful for that social media doesn't provide.	FREE SPACE	Create a playlist of five songs that represent your personality without researching trends.	Think of a challenge you overcame, and write about how it shaped who you are today.
Write down how you feel when you take a break from social media.	Reflect on how you felt after you completed a non electronic self care activity.	Name a time you and a friend or family member enjoyed free time without social media	List your top three experiences or vacation spots you will travel to and wouldn't get on social media to vlog.	Name a time you made a family member or friend laugh or happy in person.
Write a letter to your future self about who you are now and one thing you wish you can change.	Write the lyrics of your favorite song that best describes your experiences without researching.	Think of a time when you felt confident or proud without social media validation.	Write down a positive affirmation you want to say to yourself daily, without social media influence.	Write a thank you note to someone who has had a positive impact on your life

YOU'RE MORE THAN LIKES AND FOLLOWERS!

HOW HAVE YOUR FEELINGS CHANGED OVER TIME?

Did you know it is okay to have positive or negative feelings? That is normal! Our feelings change often because there are always environmental stressors that cause our moods to change.

Environmental stressors are different types of stressors that can cause us to feel stressed and negatively impact our overall well-being.

THINK ABOUT YOUR FEELINGS.

How did you feel this morning when you woke up? How did you feel throughout the day? Did anything impact your mood? How are you feeling right in this moment? What about last week? How was your mood?

Share your thoughts below.

**If you're ever feeling down...
Here are some ways to boost your feelings.**

- Check Your Feelings: Notice how social media makes you feel and what it might be taking time away from (like family, friends, or hobbies).

- Choose Wisely: Follow accounts that make you feel good. Mute, block, or report anyone who's rude, fake, or stressful, and tell a trusted adult if needed.

- Set Time Rules: Decide with friends when to be online and when to take breaks, like at night.

- Talk About It: Share what you see with adults. They can help with the good and the not-so-good parts.

- Find Good Friends: Be online with people who support you and treat others kindly, not those who bully or post hurtful things.

Can you think of *ONE* more?

_____

_____

_____

_____

MY AFFIRMATION WALL

"I'm just a kid who loves social media."

- I matter, even if I don't post today.
- My smile is real, and that's enough.
- I am awesome just being me.
- I do not need likes to feel loved.
- I can do anything I put my mind to.
- I have a big heart and big dreams.
- Offline, I am somebody.
- I love myself, and I will be the best version of myself.
- I am confident that I can use social media safely.
- I control my actions, and it doesn't control me.
- I'm growing every day, even if no one sees it online.
- My real friends like me for who I am, not my post.
- I am kind to others and myself.

SPOT THE FAKE!

Can you tell the difference between the pictures below? Write "real" or "fake" under each picture based on what you think. Which picture is edited? Which picture is real?

_____   _____

Which do you think is real? Why? How does each photo make you feel? Would you feel different if you found out the "perfect" photo was fake or edited?

YOU ARE REAL, AND THAT'S POWERFUL!

Social media is full of people filtering their photos and editing their pictures. People typically only show their best memories and do not show when they're going through tough times.

But REAL people have REAL feelings, REAL issues, REAL flaws, and REAL stories. And guess what? That is what makes you powerful.

You do not have to be "perfect" or filter your photos to be amazing. You are amazing for showing up each day at school, even when you do not want to. Or how about doing your chores at home, even though you don't want to do that, either?

Just know …

It's easy to look at someone else's picture online and think they have a perfect life. But online, we do not always see their full life. Someone might post a smiling selfie, but deep inside, they may be sad or having a hard day. A nice beach vacation post doesn't show the boring or lonely moments while they are lying down under the sun at the beach, and a weekend vlog post won't show how angry someone was that they got in trouble at school, and their parents fussed at them.

When you compare your life to someone else's reel or pictures posted on social media, you might start feeling like you're not good enough or you don't live the best life. But the truth is, you are already enough, and you still have time to develop the life you want to live. Your real, growing self is more powerful than a fake version of someone else's post.

And remember ...

The number of followers you have and the likes you get do not determine your self-worth. It does not matter how perfect your photos look. It is more important to have good morals, make good grades in school, and have good behavior. Your realness is enough!

Let's do some reflection!

One thing I like about my real self is: _____

One thing people don't see online about me is:

_____

One thing that makes me different:

_____

One thing I will not post on social media is:

_____

REAL VS. FAKE

Read each statement carefully and decide if you're being REAL or FAKE by the actions listed below. Put a check mark by the one that feels most like you.

STATEMENT	REAL	FAKE
Telling the truth and putting my real age on my social media profile.		
Using someone else picture as your profile picture		
Likes, views, and comments determine my worth and physical attractiveness		
My follower count does NOT determine if I am important, liked, or worthy of living my best life.		
Everyone on social media is always happy and perfect.		
I feel better about myself because of social media.		
Social media is NOT the only way to make friends.		
People will forget about me if I do not post regularly.		
If I get a negative comment, that means I am doing something wrong and people do not like me.		

MY WORLD, MY RULES!

IF YOU COULD CREATE THE PERFECT WORLD, WHAT WOULD IT LOOK LIKE?

What would your world look like if YOU were in charge? Would it be kind, creative, loving, and full of real connection with real people?

In this part of the workbook, you get to dream BIG and I mean BIG. I want you to design a world that makes you feel comfortable, safe, fun, and full of self-love, both online and offline.

Following celebrities, influencers, content creators, or just other "normal" people on social media can sometimes make us feel like we have to fit in, follow trends, or be or look perfect. But in your world, you get to decide what really matters.

THIS ACTIVITY HELPS YOU:

- Think about what's real vs. fake or what's just for likes
- Imagine a place where everyone feels confident and loved, and no one is left out
- Set your own rules for kindness, safety, and self-respect
- Build a world that supports your mental health and happiness

Your perfect world starts with knowing who you are and what makes you feel proud to be you.

READY TO DESIGN IT? LET'S GO!

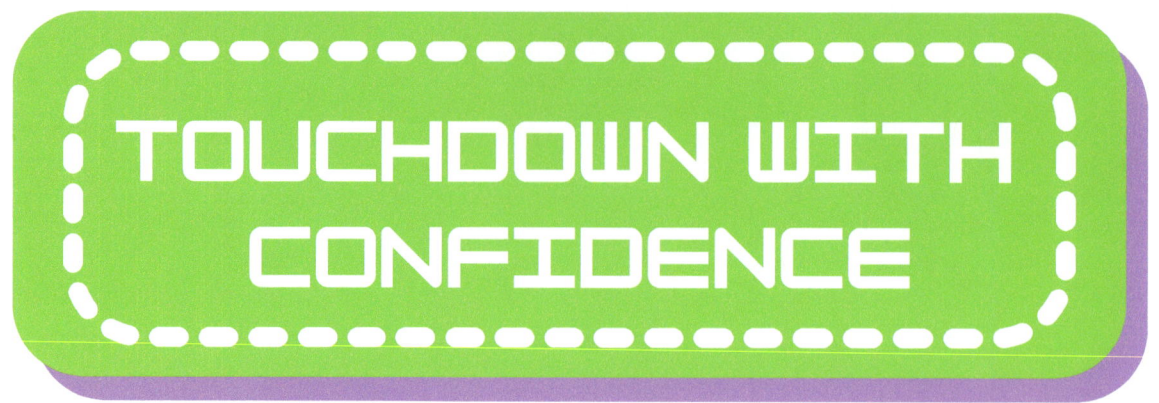

TOUCHDOWN WITH CONFIDENCE

If social media were to end today, would you still be important? You would still be powerful and have great value to give. You don't need likes, follows, or filters to be amazing. Your smile, ideas, talents, and kindness are what make you unique and different. You being your true self is special.

YOU ARE POWERFUL!

On the next page, help your player make a touchdown with confidence by guiding them through the football field maze. Along the way, they'll pass through positive maze checkpoints and online obstacles to avoid!

MAZE CHECKPOINTS

POSITIVE POST
Write something kind or encouraging.

BOUNDARIES ZONE
SAY "NO" TO SOMETHING THAT DOESN'T FEEL RIGHT.

FAKE FILTERS

DRAMA POSTS

REAL FRIENDS ONLY
Follow people who make you feel good.

OFFLINE TIME-OUT
Take a break from the screen and do something fun!

COMPARISON ZONES

DRAMA COMMENTS

SELF-TALK SIDELINE
Say one great thing about yourself.

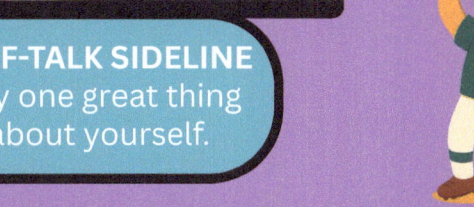

SELF-ESTEEM & MOOD TRACKER

Let's track your mood to see how you are feeling after learning about the topics in this lesson:

Check the circle that describes how you feel right now.

Did you use social media today: (Yes or No) _____

How did it make me feel? _____

Let's track your self-esteem to see how you feel about yourself and your confidence: *Circle which best describes you.*

- I feel good about myself.
- I feel unsure.
- I compared myself to others.
- I feel proud of something I did.
- I didn't feel like "enough" today.

CHAPTER 6

UNPLUG AND CELEBRATE ME!

CUT IT OFF

You have made it to the last lesson of this workbook. You're almost done, and it's almost time to celebrate yourself. But before we celebrate, remember a few important things we talked about throughout this workbook:

It is okay to take time away from your electronic devices, especially social media.

When you take a break, enjoy a hobby away from devices.

Set strong boundaries when using social media.

Stay safe, and always tell an adult if you do not feel comfortable with anything you see or hear.

If you ever start feeling upset, take a step back and do something calming. And again, if you ever feel sad, remember to tell an adult, and you can always read through this workbook again.

KEEP IT POSITIVE!

BRAIN BREAK

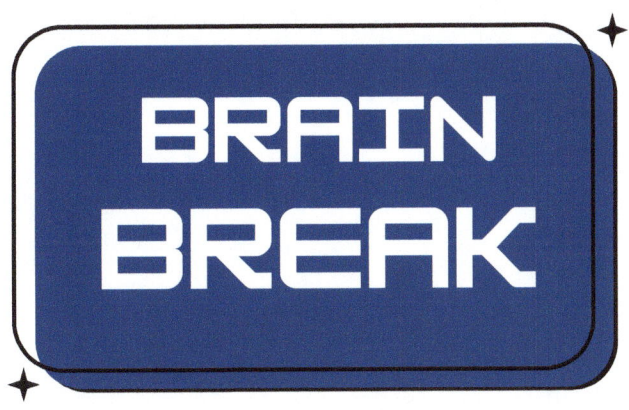

Draw a picture of two things you want to cut out from your negative online habits.

MY VOICE MATTERS!

Did you know that every time you post, comment, or share, you're using your voice? And how you use it matters. Are you spreading kindness or causing harm? Social media can be a powerful tool to express yourself, stand up for what's right, and inspire others. Don't stay silent or just follow the crowd. Your voice can create change and show the world how amazing you are.

Have you ever wanted to speak up online but didn't?

How can you use your voice to make someone's day better?

What does it mean to speak up in a kind and respectful way?

LET'S HEAR YOUR VOICE

LET'S REALLY HEAR HOW YOU CAN USE YOUR VOICE TO SPREAD KINDNESS.

Make up a song, rap, or poem with at least *six* lines. Use positive words that can help someone feel better or show the world how awesome you are. You can do this by yourself or with a friend.

_____

_____

_____

_____

_____

_____

_____

WALKING TRAIL

Have you ever walked on a beach or in mud and noticed the footprints you leave behind? Posting, liking, or sharing online works the same way. You're leaving a digital footprint. Even if you delete it, screenshots or archives can keep it around.

Your digital footprint shows the trail of who you are online. Some footprints spread kindness, positivity, and fun memories. Others can leave a negative mark, like mean jokes or rude comments.

BEFORE POSTING, ASK YOURSELF:
- *Would I want my teacher, parent, or future self to see this?*
- *Is it kind, respectful, and true to me?*
- *Does it build up others or tear them down?*

Your choices shape how people see you and how you see yourself. Make sure your footprints are ones you're proud of.

MY DIGITIAL FOOTPRINT

Let's have a discussion.

1. Positive things I want to be known for online

2. Words I want others to think of when they see my posts

3. One message I would want my future self to see

4. One way I can use my voice in a good way online

5. A motivating comment for someone who is having a sad day

PLUG IN
SELF-CARE = SELF-LOVE

Self-care means caring for your feelings, health, happiness, future, and success the same way you would care for a good friend.

When you scroll on social media, it's easy to forget about yourself. You might start comparing your life to others, trying too hard to get "likes," or even acting in ways that don't feel like the real you.

That's why self-care matters. It reminds you to pause, treat yourself kindly, and focus on the things that make you feel good inside and out.

THINGS TO REMEMBER:

- Take breaks from your screen so your mind can rest.
- Go back to hobbies you love, like drawing, music, or sports.
- Say kind things to yourself, even if no one else does.
- Try something new: a skill, a recipe, or a fun project.
- Remember, not everything online is true. Trust what feels real.

80

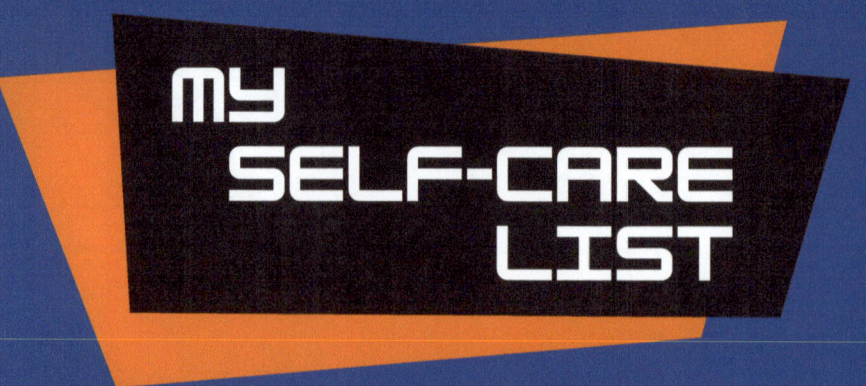

MY SELF-CARE LIST

Let's create a self-care list.

This activity will be very useful. You can always go back to this list if you need to remember things to do to start loving yourself more. Be kind to yourself! We all make mistakes, and no one is perfect. But one thing you are is IMPORTANT!

Something that helps me relax: _____

Something that moves my body: _____

Something kind I say to myself: _____

Something I do to rest: _____

Something creative I enjoy: _____

One way I take a break from screens: _____

Something that makes me feel proud: _____

One person who makes me feel loved: _____

Remember: You already matter. Practicing good self-care is a way to show self-love and to boost your self-esteem.

MY ONLINE SAFETY TIPS
Be Smart! Be Kind! Protect Your Peace!

SET HEALTHY BOUNDARIES

- Never share your full name, address, or personal information online.
- Set time limits for screen time.
- You don't have to respond to every message.
- It's okay to walk away!
- Only gain a "real" connection with people you know in real life, not through online gaming and social media. Just because you met them online, they are not your friend!

SPOT THE RED FLAGS

- Someone you don't know keeps asking personal questions
- You're confused or feel uncomfortable about a comment or message
- Someone keeps telling you to send them a picture
- Someone is telling you to click a link that looks weird (It's a scam!)

KNOW WHEN TO ASK FOR HELP

- If something online makes you feel scared, confused, or upset, talk to a trusted adult right away.
- Trusted adults can be your parents, teachers, counselors, or another grown-up who listens and helps.

You will not get in trouble for speaking up about something that made you uncomfortable. If something doesn't feel or sound right, then it isn't right. Trust your gut and tell a trusting adult!

MY UNPLUGGED ACTIVITIES LIST

10 FUN THINGS YOU CAN DO WITHOUT A SCREEN

1. Create and design a comic book!

2. Enjoy a physical activity: i.e, running, walking, swimming

3. Build something with blocks, Legos, sticks, cardboard, or pretty much anything

4. Make an activities jar: put cool things in the jar and pull something out when you get bored

5. Make something cool and new: i.e, recipe, video game, playbook for your favorite sport, painting/drawing, or bracelets

6. Listen to your favorite music and have a dance party

7. Write a poem or a song

8. Play a card or board game

9. Start a collection, i.e., sports cards, state quarters, bottle tops, stickers, leaves, shells, etc..

10. Host a talent show or DIY a science experiment

LET'S DISCUSS!

Would you try any of these? Can you think of any more unplugged activities to add to this list?

THE ROAD TO 'UNPLUG AND PLUG IN'

Riding your bike on a new road can be scary, but with a trusted adult, they are there to guide you and keep you safe. Unplugging from screens is a lot like that. It might make you feel like you're missing out, but taking a break from screens to reconnect with what matters, YOU, is important!

ALWAYS REMEMBER!

"Unplugging" doesn't mean throwing away your phone or never going online again. It simply means you're making a good decision to step away from the screens for a little while, allowing your mind and heart to relax, refocus, and recharge.

When you unplug from the screen, you get to plug into something even better than social media: YOU!

It may look like:
- Drawing, dancing, or building something awesome.
- Reading or writing your own story.
- Playing outside, card or board games, or hanging out with friends.
- Learning something new (a recipe, a magic trick, or a sport)

Just like your tablet, cell phone, or gaming controller. Your electronic devices need time to recharge after you have been using them for a few hours.

When you unplug, you give yourself space to rest, think, create, and connect with things and people that make you feel good inside, strong, and confident. You sleep better at night, protect your eyes and focus better, and feel less stressed.

Unplugging gives you time to do the things that make you the best version of you!

SELF-ESTEEM & MOOD TRACKER

Let's track your mood to see how you are feeling after learning about the topics in this lesson:

Check the circle that describes how you feel right now.

Did you use social media today: (Yes or No) _____

How did it make me feel? _____

Let's track your self-esteem to see how you feel about yourself and your confidence: *Circle which best describes you.*

- I feel good about myself.
- I feel unsure.
- I compared myself to others.
- I feel proud of something I did.
- I didn't feel like "enough" today.

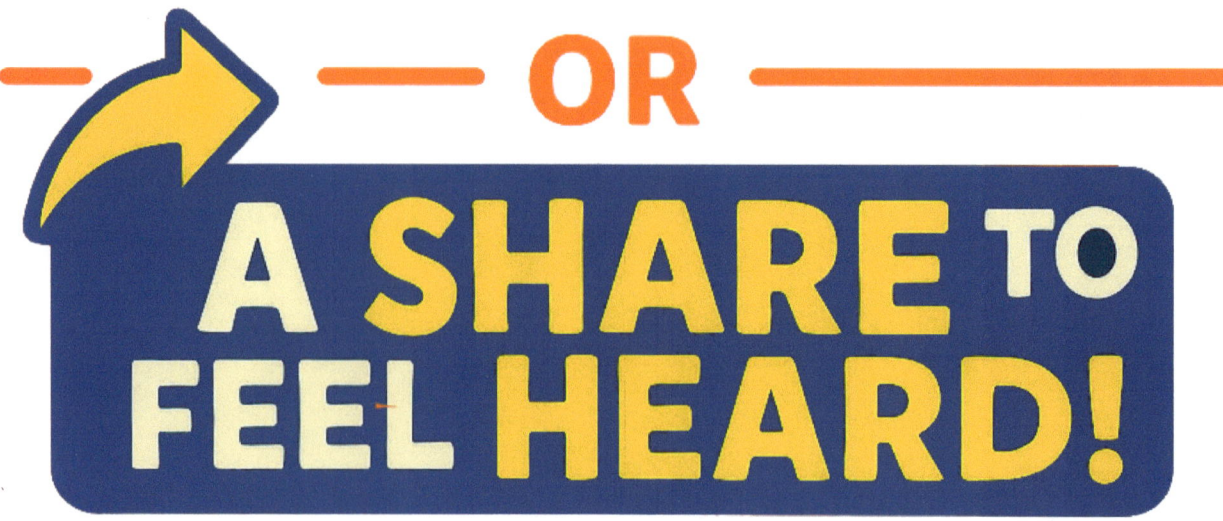

CONGRATULATIONS
YOU DID IT!

You finished all the lessons in this workbook, and that's a big deal! You've learned a lot, grown a ton, and picked up some amazing new skills. Go ahead, give yourself a pat on the back!

Now, you know how to stay safe online, set boundaries, walk away from negative stuff, and feel good about who you are, with or without social media.

YOU'VE LEARNED THAT:

- Likes and followers don't show your worth.
- You don't need filters to be amazing.
- You are enough just by being YOU!
- You can be real, kind, and confident in a social media world.

It may not have been easy, but you did the work, and that's something to be super proud of. Keep using the skills you learned, and remember: Your future self will thank you.

GREAT JOB! Now, go shine bright and show the world just how awesome you are, online and offline!

SOCIAL MEDIA & SELF-ESTEEM POST-TEST

Fill in the blank with the best word or idea that fits. Do your best, there are no wrong answers!

1. One way I can protect myself online is by setting healthy _____ with people I talk to on social media.
2. Social media can be fun, but it can also affect the way I feel about my _____.
3. It's important to take breaks from my phone or gaming system so I can take care of my _____ and feelings.
4. Before I post something online, I should ask myself if it is _____ and _____.
5. When someone is being mean or hurtful online, that is called _____.
6. Not everything I see on social media is real. Some pictures are edited or _____ to look perfect.
7. Being kind online is called using good _____.
8. I can tell if a person is trustworthy online by looking for _____ signs and thinking carefully before I share anything.
9. The digital world means everything I do online leaves a _____, so I should always think before I click.

10. If there were no social media, I would spend more time _____ or doing things like _____.
11. When I feel left out or jealous of something I see on social media, I can help myself feel better by _____.
12. I know I am being true to myself online when I post things that make me feel _____ and _____.
13. If a stranger messages me online and it feels uncomfortable, I should _____ and talk to a trusted _____.
14. Social media doesn't show the full story of someone's life, so I remind myself not to _____ myself to others online.
15. Being confident online means I don't need to post just to get _____ or _____.

MY WORKBOOK REFLECTION

Complete this activity, and think about what you learned in this workbook.

1. What was your pre-test score?   What is your post-test score?

   _____   _____

2. How do you feel about your two scores? What does it tell you?

   _____

   _____

3. While using this workbook, did you grow in your knowledge about boosting self-esteem while using social media, or learn something new? (Yes or No?) _____

   If yes, what did you learn or like most about this workbook?

   _____

4. What is one thing you can change now about your online habits?

   _____

5. One word that describes how I feel after this workbook:

   _____

SCORING GUIDE FOR PRE/POST-TEST

Q#	Topic	Key Concept to Look For	Examples of Acceptable Answers
1	Setting Boundaries	Understanding limits	Boundaries, rules, saying "no"
2	Social Media & Self-Esteem	Awareness about self-image	Self, confidence, emotions, feelings
3	Taking Breaks from Technology	Knowing when to walk away	Mind, brain, emotions, feelings, health
4	Online Etiquette	Thoughtfulness & kindness	Kind, true, respectful, nice, helpful
5	Cyberbullying	Negative online behavior	Bullying, cyberbullying, being mean
6	Fake vs. Real Content	Understanding edited pictures	Edited, fake, photoshopped, not true
7	Digital Manners	Kindness and respect	Kindness, manners, respect
8	Trust & Safety Online	Trust and being safe	Red flags, warning signs, trusted adult
9	Permanent Online Actions	Awareness about online act	Footprint, trace, history, track, record
10	Life Beyond Social Media	Imagination & the real world	Playing, sports, drawing, hobbies, etc.
11	Coping with Negative Feelings	How to self-soothe	Take a break, talk to someone, unplug
12	Self-Expression & Confidence	Being your authentic self	Happy, proud, confident, real, myself
13	Online Danger/Strangers	Smart & safe choices	Ignore, block, report, tell a trusted adult
14	Comparing Online Lives	Reality check	Compare, judge, feel bad, be jealous
15	Validation vs. Self-Worth	Confidence check	Likes, followers, attention, comments

SCORING GUIDE:

- **11–15 points:** Excellent understanding! The student shows strong awareness and can apply ideas from the workbook.

- **7–10 points:** Good progress! Some understanding is shown, with room for further discussion and practice.

- **0–6 points:** Emerging awareness. More guided conversations and examples may help this student grow.

ANSWER KEY

Think Before You Post! Word Search

M	N	G	V	H	T	N	A	X	M	G	S	W	F	Y
O	C	K	T	S	A	O	U	Y	U	C	S	R	C	D
J	M	G	I	N	G	W	F	F	L	Q	J	S	Q	P
K	E	P	A	N	F	O	V	F	O	U	A	K	A	Y
I	S	H	Q	X	D	R	Y	O	Q	F	W	D	R	D
A	S	V	S	D	X	N	Y	E	E	W	W	C	S	P
E	A	N	U	Y	G	U	E	T	L	D	I	H	C	R
Q	G	Z	U	X	T	K	Y	S	E	D	A	V	F	O
O	E	O	J	O	L	H	B	Z	S	R	M	X	M	S
F	S	C	S	J	I	P	I	L	I	B	D	B	H	L
F	S	R	A	P	K	V	V	N	O	F	V	O	Y	F
I	G	J	U	X	E	Y	G	W	K	C	C	M	R	Y
O	P	P	K	A	S	V	T	R	S	V	V	K	X	D
X	C	E	Y	R	V	F	H	O	A	H	E	V	R	U
R	E	S	P	E	C	T	V	H	O	D	N	Y	B	F

Unscramble Words

1. PPYHA happy
2. ASD sad
3. ASINXUO anxious
4. AGYRN angry
5. CEFDNTION confident
6. YDRNEFLI friendly
7. SDSEERST stressed
8. OUHRM humor
9. AXELR relax
10. OELVD loved
11. NINETACUR uncertain
12. ERNUCIES insecure
13. EMWDLHEOERV overwhelm
14. EIRDROW worried
15. LETF TOU left out
16. ULEFHCER cheerful
17. SSEESTDR UTO stressed ou
18. AONTADIV avoidant
19. OELNLY lonely
20. DERBO bored
21. CMLA calm
22. BREAV brave
23. ETCDIEX excited
24. SPATDNPDEIOI disappointe
25. SRSUPEDRI surprised

Game Time, Guess Who? Confidence vs. Self-Esteem

1. Confidence
2. Self-Esteem
3. Confidence
4. Self-Esteem

Spot the Fake

1. Fake
2. Real

*Hint: the edited image has the darker shadow

Touchdown of Confidence Maze Checkpoints

Play Nice: Crossword Puzzle

1. Break
2. Forever
3. Settings
4. Nice
5. Adult
6. Block
7. Cyberbullying
8. Etiquette
9. Think
10. Gossiping
11. Safe
12. Strengths
13. Respect
14. Report
15. Kindness

CONGRATULATIONS

THIS CERTIFICATE OF COMPLETION IS PROUDLY PRESENTED TO

_____

For completing all the chapters in the

Unplug and Plug In:
A Fun Guide to Boost Your Self-Esteem
in a Social Media World

_____

Dr. Shanika Thomas, LCSW

REFERENCE PAGE

American Academy of Pediatrics. (n.d.). Impact of social media on youth. Center of Excellence on Social Media and Youth Mental Health. Retrieved June 4, 2025, from https://www.aap.org/en/patient-care/media-and-children/center-of-excellence-on-social-media-and-youth-mental-health/qa-portal/qa-portal-library/qa-portal-library-questions/impact-of-social-media-on-youth/

Dhingra, M., & Mudgal, R. K. (2019, March 15). Historical evolution of social media: An overview. Paper presented at the International Conference on Advances in Engineering Science Management & Technology (ICAESMT), Uttaranchal University, Dehradun, India. https://doi.org/10.2139/ssrn.3395665

How to Raise Resilient Kids in the Digital Age: Preventing "Strawberry Generations" - Teknos. https://www.teknos.my.id/2024/03/how-to-raise-resilient-kids-in-digital_7.html

Protecting Your Child's Online Privacy with Kaspersky Safe Kids - ICT Distribution - Pakistan. https://ictdistribution.net/pk/protecting-your-childs-online-privacy-with-kaspersky-safe-kids/

ABOUT THE AUTHOR
DR. SHANIKA THOMAS, LCSW

A Licensed Clinical Social Worker and school social worker born in Conway, SC, is also the mother of a student-athlete. She began writing children's books to address the growing need for resources that help young people manage emotions. Dr. Thomas earned her B.A. in Psychology and Master of Social Work from Clark Atlanta University and later a Doctorate in Social Work from Capella University.

In addition to working with students, she provides clinical supervision to professionals pursuing licensure, shaping the next generation of social workers. With years of experience in clinical and school settings, Dr. Thomas supports children and teens individually and in groups, partnering with parents to promote academic and personal success. She is also a social media influencer who uses her platform to inspire confidence, encourage self-care, and uplift others. She lives in Metro Atlanta, where she enjoys motherhood, fitness, traveling, and shopping.

www.ingramcontent.com/pod-product-compliance
Lightning Source LLC
Chambersburg PA
CBHW041520070526
44585CB00002B/20